HEAVEN & OTHER POEMS

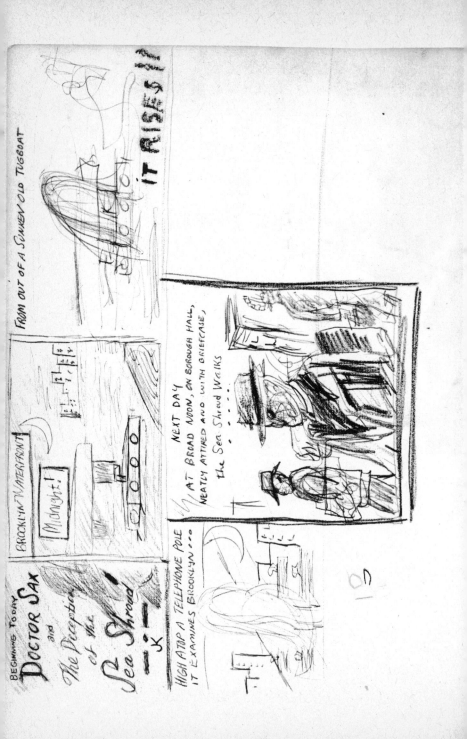

Jack Kerouac

HEAVEN

&
Other Poems

GREY FOX PRESS
San Francisco

Cover photograph of Jack Kerouac taken by Carolyn Cassady
in 1952.

Frontispiece: "Doctor Sax and the Sea Shroud," Jack Kerouac's
comic strip drawn for the Cassady children in 1952 or 1953.

Library of Congress Cataloging in Publication Data

Kerouac, John, 1922–1969
    Heaven & other poems.

  I. Title.
PS3521.E735H4   1977   811'.5'4   77-6233
ISBN 0-912516-30-5
ISBN 0-912516-31-3 pbk.

Sixth printing, 1992.

Distributed by Subco
P.O. Box 168
Monroe, OR 97456

CONTENTS

EDITOR'S NOTE

Although I had had some editorial experience of Jack Kerouac's *On the Road* as early as 1954 and 1955, when I had copyedited the "Jazz of the Beat Generation" episode for *New World Writing*, and had read the whole ms for a publisher, I did not get to meet him until late November or early December of 1957 when he and Allen Ginsberg came to my apartment at 59 West 9th Street in the Village. At the time I was putting together the second, "San Francisco Scene," issue of *Evergreen Review*, and Allen and Jack gave me mss and filled me in on recent developments on the West Coast.

During the next two years Jack sent me poems for *Evergreen Review* and for the anthology, *The New American Poetry*, I was editing in 1959. In the end we decided to print choruses from *Mexico City Blues* chosen by Allen plus Jack's biographical note and brief statement of his poetics. Later, in 1961, when I'd moved to San Francisco, Jack sent me his *San Francisco Blues* for a projected volume which never got off the ground.

His Mémère, Gabrielle, I first met when Barney Rosset entertained Jack and his mother and his French editors, Claude Gallimard and Michel Mohrt, at a luncheon party in 1958. And in the late spring of 1959, when I'd returned from a trip through South America, I accepted Jack's invitation and traveled to Northport for an overnight visit. Jack showed me his writing room and we talked at length about his unpublished mss and the origins of the Beat Generation. Mémère served a delicious and hearty supper which we ate at a round captain's table in the comfortable kitchen. Jack and I made a short foray to a nearby liquor store and bar and then we all turned in at a fairly early hour, they to watch TV in their bedrooms and I to sleep in the guest room.

This book belatedly collects the poems Jack sent me and his letters and statements regarding his verse.

Donald Allen
May 1977

HEAVEN & OTHER POEMS

From SAN FRANCISCO BLUES

[1]

San Francisco is too sad
Time, I cant understand
Fog, shrouds the hills in
Makes unshod feet so cold
Pity the poor Pomo, St. Francis & the birds,
Fills black rooms with day
Dayblack in the white windows
And gloom in the pain of pianos;
Shadows in the jazz age
Filing by; ladders of flappers
Painters' white bucket
Funny 3 Stooge Comedies
And fuzzy headed Hero
Moofle Lip suck't it all up
And wondered why
The milk & cream of heaven
Was writ in gold leaf
On a book—big eyes

[2]

For the world
The better to see——
And big lips for the word
And Buddhahood
And death.
Touch the cup to these sad lips
Let the purple grape foam
In my gullet deep
Spread saccharine
And crimson carnadine
In my vine of veins
And shoot power
To my hand
Belly heart & head——
   This Magic Carpet
   Arabian World
   Will take us
   Easeful Zinging
   Cross the Sky
   Singing Madrigals
   To horizons of golden
   Moment emptiness
Whither whence uncaring

MACDOUGAL STREET BLUES

In the Form of 3 Cantos

CANTO UNO

The goofy foolish
   human parade
Passing on Sunday
   art streets
Of Greenwich Village

Pitiful drawings of
   images on an
   iron fence
   ranged there
      by self believing
      artists
      with no hair
      and black berets
      showing green seas
      eating at rock
      and Pleiades
      of Time

Pestiferating at moon squid
   Salt flat tip fly toe
      tat sand traps
With cigar smoking interesteds
   puffing at the
      stroll
I mean sincerely
   naive sailors buying prints
Women with red banjos

On their handbags
    And arts handicrafty
        Slow shuffling
        art-ers of Washington Square
        Passing in what they think
        Is a happy June afternoon
Good God the Sorrow
    They dont even listen to me when
        I try to tell them they will die

They say "Of course I know
I'll die, Why shd you mention
It now—Why should I worry
About it—It ll happen
It ll happen—Now
I want a good time—
Excuse me—
It's a beautiful happy June
Afternoon I want to walk in—

Why are you so tragic & gloomy?
And in the corner at the
        Pony Stables
On Sixth Ave & 4th
Sits Bodhisattva Meditating
In Hobo Rags
    Praying at Joe Gould's chair
For the Emancipation

Of the shufflers passing by,
Immovable in Meditation
He offers his hand & feet
    To the passers by
And nobody believes

That there's nothing to believe in.
Listen to Me.
There is no sidewalk artshow
    No strollers are there

No poem here, no June
    afternoon of Oh
But only Imagelessness
Unrepresented on the iron fence
Of bald artists
With black berets
    Passing by
    One moment less than this
Is future Nothingness Already

The Chess men are silent, assembled
    Ready for funny war—
        Voices of Washington Square Blues
        Rise to my Bodhisattva Poem
            Window
        I will describe them:-
            Ey t k ey ee
            Sa la o s o
            F   r   u   p   t   u r t

Etc.
No need, no words to
                describe
The sound of ignorance—
They are strolling to
                their death
Watching the Pictures of Hell
Eating Ice Cream
                of Ignorance
On wood sticks

That were once sincere
   in trees—
But I cant write, poetry,
   just prose

       * * *

I mean
   This is prose
      Not poetry
         But I want
            To be sincere

CANTO DOS

While overhead is the perfect blue
      emptiness of the sky
   With its imaginary balloons
      of false sight
   Flying around in it
      like Tathagata Flying Saucers
These poor ignorant things
      mill on sidewalks
Looking at pitiful pictures
      of what they think

Is reality
And one
      a Negro with curls
Even has a camera
      to photograph
The pictures
And Jelly Roll Man
Pops his Billy Bell
   Good Humor for sale—

W Somerset Maugham
      is on my bed

An ignorant storyteller
     millionaire queer
But Ezra Pound
     he crazy—
As the perfect sky
     beginninglessly pure
Thinglessly perfect
     waits already
They pass in multiplicity

Parade among Images
    Images Images Looking
      Looking—
And everybody's turning around
     & pointing—
Nobody looks up
    and In
Nor listens to Samantabhadra's
    Unceasing Compassion

No Sound Still
      S s s s t t
      Seethe
      Of Sea Blue Moon
      Holy X-Jack
        Miracle
        Night—
      Instead yank & yucker
      For pits & pops

Look for crashes
  Pictures
   Squares

Explosions
   Birth
    Death
    Legs
I know, sweet hero,
Enlightenment has Come
    Rest in Still

In the Sun Think
  Think Not
Think no more Lines—
Straw hat, hands a back
    Classed
He exam in atein distinct
   Rome prints—
Trees prurp
   and saw

The Chessplayers Wont End
  Still they sit
   Millions of hats
In underwater foliage
  Over marble games
   The Greeks of Chess
    Plot the Pop
   of Mate
    King Queen

—I know their game,
  their elephant with the pillar
With the pearl in it,
   Their gory bishops
   And Vital Pawns—
    Their devout frontline
    Sacrificial pawn shops
    Their stately King

Who is so tall
    Their Virgin Queens
        Pree ing to Knave
        The Night Knot
—Their Bhagavad Gitas
    of Ignorance,
    Krishna's advice,

Comma,
The game begins—
  But hidden Buddha
  Nowhere to be seen
        But everywhere
        In air atoms
        In balloon atoms
        In imaginary sight atoms
        In people atoms

In people atoms
Again
        In image atoms
        In me & you atoms
        In atom bone atoms
        Like the sky
            Already Waits
            For us eyes open to
            —Pawn fell

Horse reared
  Mate Kiked Cattle
  And Boom! Cop
  Shot Bates—
Cru put Two—
    Out—I cried—
Pound Pomed—
    Jean-Louis
        Go home, Man

I mean.——
   As solid as anything
      Is this reality of images
      In the imageless essence,
      Neither of em 11 quit
      ——So tho I am wise
      I have to wait like
         Anyotherfool

CANTO TRES

Lets forget the strollers
   Forget the scene
Lets close our eyes
   Let me instruct   Thee
            Here is dark Milk
            Here is our Sweet Mahameru
               Who will Coo
               To you Too

As he did to me
One night at three
When I w k e   i t
      P l e e
Knelt to See
Realit ee
   And I said
   'Wilt thou protect me
       for 'ver?'

And he in his throatless
   deep mother hole
   Replied ' H o m '
   (Pauvre Ange)
Mahameru

                Tathagata of Mercy
See
  He
    Now
        In dark escrow

In the middleless dark
of eyelids' lash obliviso
   So
     Among rains of Transcendent
          Pity
   Abides since Ever
        Before Evermore ness
Or thusness Imagined
O Maha Meru

O Mountain Sumeru
    O Mountain of Gold
      O Holy Gold
          O Room of Gold
            O Sweet peace
                rememberance
              O Nava lit yuku

Of sweet cactus
  Thorn of No Time
—Ply me on ward
  like boat
      thru this Sea
    Safe to Shore
    Ulysses never Sore
—Bless me Gerard
    Bless thee, Living

I shall pray for all
   sentient human
   & otherwise sentient
   beings here & everywhere
   now—
No names
 Not even faces
   One Pity
    One Milk
     One Lovelight
         s a v e

June 26 1955

From ORIZABA BLUES

[1]

Lost me Juju beads in the woods
And stood on dry stumps
        and looked around
And Lightning Creek morely roared
And wow the wild Jack Mountain
Abominable Snowman rooted
        in a stump
Even throwing football shadow
When games is ranging in the sky
Ah Gary,—would sweet Japan
Her gardens allay me
And make end sweet perfidy
—Full belly make you say
                        nice things—
When rice bowl filled, Buddha frown
I' the West, because Wall of China
Has no holds

Holdfast to temple mountain chain
Throw away the halfdollars
Big and round, & wad of gum,
And flashlight lamp—& paint—
Go be shaved head monster
In a cave—No, tea ceremony
Beneath a sweet pine tree
            (Oi?)

[2]

In Egypt under rosebushes
Fifi's fruits & sweets

My Egyptian connection's
Gonna be late, the conductor
Wouldnt take my change

The Egyptian conductor
Wouldnt nod

Sandalwood and piss and pulque
Burning in every door,
Mighty Marabuda River
Flows along

Sampans and river thieves
And woodsplitters and blind
Thieves' Markets & imbeciles
"See Milan and see the world"

Heppatity the twat kid
Hatted by the racetrack
Horses' moon barns
Spun on a gibbee
For lying alone

[3]

Eternally the lightning runs
Through form after form formless
In positive and negative repose

It makes no difference that your uncle
Was black with sufferance & bile,
The whild childscriming skies will
Always be the muchacho same

Much words been written about it
The message from infinite
That will be was brought to us
Is one
But because it has no name
We can only call it Bibit
    "It was Liebernaut who had
    the dream of uncovering Carthage"
The snow in the sea mountains

THE SEA SHROUD

(A description of my last cartoon)

The Sea Shroud comes out of a slip
    of water in Brooklyn Harbor, night,
    it emerges from a submerged tug
    right from the enamel underwear
    of the pilot's cabin

Right through up comes the shroud head,
    a draining drape of wet weedy
    watery sea net spray, ephemeral,
    climbing to knock knees against the bow
    and make the bit on the dock

And come on vanishing instead
    reappearing as a Man
    with a briefcase, on Borough Hall,
    saying nothing with a watery face
    saying nothing with an ogoo mouth

Saying nothing with a listening nose,
    saying nothing with a questionmark mouth,
    saying nothing, the briefcase full
    of seaweed—what happens to floating
    bonds when they get in the hand of the drape

Sea Shroud, turning Chinese Food to seaweed
    in his all-abominable bag, Shroud
    the taker of widows' monies in red allies
    of shame & stagedoors, purple lagoon
    Goon Shroud departs gloving the money

Earlier in the day he'd perched atop a
    flagpole in a parking lot
    on the waterfront, and looked around
    to see which way Borough Hall
    which way the little white doves

A HAIKU

The little worm
    lowers itself from the roof
By a self shat thread

MY GANG

Part One

Many people have been frighted & died in cemeteries
      since the days of my gang, the night
      Zap Plouffe came up & talked to me
      on the block and I rowed the imaginary
      horse on the rowel of the porch rail

Where I killed 700,000 flies or more
      while Ma and Blanche gossiped
      in the kitchen, and while drape sheets
      we airing on the line that's connected
      to midnight by midnight riding roses

Oy—the one bad time that Zaggo
      got home from school late, dark
      in the streets, the sisters majestico
      blooming in the alley retreat, beat,
      'Your gang is upstairs' says my mother

And I go up to my closed smoky door
      and open it to a miniature poolhall
      where all the gang is smoking & yakking
      with little cue sticks and blue chalk
      around a miniature table on stilts

Bets being made, spittings out the window,
      cold out there, old murder magoon
      the winter man in my tree has seen
      to it that inhalator autumn
      prestidigitate on time & in ripe form,
      to wit cold

To wit cold, to wit you, to wit winter
To wit time, to wit bird, to wit dust—
      That was some game ole Lousy blanged
      When he beat G.J. that time,
      and Artaud roared

Part Two

Artaud was the cookie that was always
    in my hair, a ripe screaming tight
    brother with heinous helling neck-veins
    who liked to riddle my fantasms
    with yaks of mocksqueak joy

'Why dont you like young Artaud?'
    always I'm asked, because he boasts
    and boasts, brags, brags, ya, ya, ya,
    because he's crazy because he's mad
    and because he never gives us a chance to talk

Awright——I'd like to know what
Billy's got against me——But he wont
tell, and it's brother deep——In the room
they're shooting the break, clack,
the little balls break, scatter di mania,

They take aim on little balls and break
    em up to fall, in plicky pockpockets
    for little children's names drawing
    pictures in the games in the whistle
    of the old corant tree splashing

In the mighty mu Missouri lame image
    of time and again the bride & groom,
    boom & again the bidal bood, oo,
    too-too and rumble o mumble thunden
    bow, ole Lousy is in my alley

Ole Lousy's my alley I'll lay it on me
    I'll shoot fourteen farthings for Father Machree
    and if ole Hotsatots dont footsie
    down here bring my gruel, I'll
    be cruel, I'll be cruel

ORLANDO BLUES: 31st Chorus

O Gary Snyder
    we work in many ways
In Montreal I suffered tile
    and rain

In Additional Christmas
    waylayed babes

In old crow Hotels
    full of blue babes
      in pink dressinggowns
          down

But O Gary Snyder,
    where'd you go,
What I meant was
    there you go

In Montreal I worked a manied-way

And, better than Old Post
    I learned t'appreciate
      in many ways
        Montreal, Soulsville,
        and Drain

A TV POEM

Tathata is Essence Isness
And I see it Akshobying
like innumerable moth lights
In the lavender plaster wall
behind the television forest of wires
in my sister's cool livingroom
the radiating isness not obliterated,
transcendentally seen, by either
white plaster or wall lavender
wingboards with bridge of black
and wires of Oh dots

Meanwhile the gray lost unturned on
    screen shows its gray black
And then the reflected window
    outdoor blob squares
Like silver shining
A TV show with me deep gloomily
    invited included in the
Slow motionless background
    where you cannot see
My white sea moving shirt
    of pencil on lap page

So that the scene is real
    a show of world
But through it all still I see
Transcendental (and hear) radiations
    from some pure and tranquil
Blank and empty center Screen
    of Mind's Immortal Ecstasy
And even Reynolds' Blue Boy
    on the wall over there

Bathed in holy day light
  Has his little black fly

Permeative with Buddhamoths
    and Buddha Lands
And his pale face with the
    Black hair cut
Sways, moves, force-weaver
    Middle way
     Middle
      W
      a
      y

Like a middle void hole
    cloud be decking
Human sad hat holding
    impression of
Dance——
      Attainer to Actual Isness
      Adoration to Your No Need to Move

        Do nothing & ye shall soon agree

HEAVEN

Like going to Xochimilco and seeing
everything with clear loving eyes,
it will be, to go to Heaven
a wise angel of the dead
among the blind unborn angels
unnumberable—
Whole buzzing areas of Heaven
will have nothing but mosquitos—

Unborn angels wont know
what they look like
but wise angels of free will
and goodness will see them,
wearing the transformation bodies
of their future death—
     We will be able to visit
dinosaurs by the millions
and have picnics among them,
of ambrosia, unmolested—
   Dead angels of evil will,
   shall be quartered
   with the Devil
   behind Golden Bars
   unable to rejoice
   for a long long time
—Judgement Day
will take place in Heaven
and really be Universal
Freeing Day—
     by this time
    nobody will need love
       any more
        except

to be Alone
with God's Face
whose Shroud I've already seen.

The Church?
Earth's dogmatic mistakes
have nothing to do with Heaven
—O Gerard! I'll see you
soon!
And Chirico!
And Christ!
May I kiss Thee, Son
of Man?
Just once?
And you, Gotama,
receive thy 83-year-old
blessing?
Okay

If this were not so
God wouldnt be God,
or Good,
God be with ye
means *Good* bye—
if it aint so
I'll make it so
by my Will.

Gerard will be a 9-year old
cutie
in Heaven
and I'll be oldern
anybody in my family
oldern my father, who'll
laugh.
Allen will be in ecstasies

Peter Amazed
Neal bleakly content
            at last
Carolyn prim
  Ma the same as now
  Leroi soft
  Lucien old & wise
  Cessa angelic
  Dody painting gates
      of Paradise
          for the holy fun
  and Hitler stroking
his mustache by the side
of Napoleonic Inventors
    of rockets,
        barred awhile

for Heaven is big enough
(it's all empty space
endless) to take in
unnumberable non-numbers
of anything & everything
that has and aint
happened all over
        anyway
      or not at all

    God Smiles

    Gee God I'm Glad
        'Bye

                    I AM
                    Dec 2 '58
                    Northport

25

(Louis Armstrong will
    blow his top)

Some of the wise angels,
the dark of the dead,
  favored in Heaven,
will shake their heads
sadly persuading certain
unborn martyrs not
to be born, but God Smiles,
and up there theres no Time
—Wow,————
I guess I'll shut up now

(Except, we will be able
to examine the huge mouths
& teeth of Dinosaurs
& they will look at us
with big sad eyes—
not to mention creatures
with or without free will
from every planet
in all the chilicosms—
even the little stem men
from Asagratamak—
There will be polite
interchange of experiences,
an endless ride)—
        When we see God's Face
We wont see anything
            else

Yes, finally
because I see it
Thru the brown grain
of this turd earth—

Who is my Witness?
     My Will!

And this is the will I leave
     to my children

Come little unborn angels,
get it over with!
Hello Thomas Hardy!
Myself I'm going to visit
endlessly the endless groves
of trees up there
and have enough time
to hug each one—
and this time they'll talk
———
     All the amores
of Spanish earth you see
were not in vain—

Girls called Angelina
for no perturbing reason.

It wont be like the hydrogen bomb
when God finally shows
  his Face, it will be sudden
          happiness,
like when you suddenly feel
     like cryin
  when you first see yr infant's
  face in its mother's arms.

This knowledge makes me
go "Ha ha ha" and
go "Oh boy" and
go "Whoopee"
because now I know

that old age is therefore
the development of angels.

Mutilated people will float
around like mutilated leaves,
more curious than the others,
    that's all

Roy Campanella will smile
& float around in Heaven
as good as John L Sullivan

The legless man no
              rollerboard—
Tiny Tim will keep screaming
    "God Bless Everyone"

Sebastian will weep.

Burnt children
    of the Chicago School Fire
  of Our Lady of the Angels
will be like little black
niggers in the Virgin Mary's
    beautiful blue & white
            golden yard
                forever.

For we all go back
where we came from,
    God's Lit Brain,
        his Transcendent Eye
of Wisdom

And there's your bloody circle
called Samsara
            by the ignorant
            Buddhists, who will

still be funny Masters
    up there, bless em.

Stella will bless Sebastian.
Zen men will devise koans
    for snakes to solve.
Rodgers & Hammerstein
will have endless hits.

Oh boy, Broadway
    will be raised at last.

Henri Cru will tell
endless stories to a billion
listeners.
Gregory Corso will dance
around with a laurel
in his hair, writing poems.

Later!
I'm gonna do it!

Phil Whalen will be
a blue cloud anytime
he wants—
Bob Donlin will stare
with endless blue eyes
out of the milk bar,
and W.C. Fields will get
his red eye—
My cats Timmy & Tyke
will always be at my side
—They wont be jealous
but make friends
with Bootsie, Kewpie,
and Davey, and Beauty

and Bob—even
the little dry moth
with the beady black eyes
can sit on my arm
        forever,
  till we all see God
when that which we love
solves & melts in one
            Glow

See?

  And the little mouse
  that I killed will devour
  me into its golden belly.
  That little mouse was God.

Dante and Beatrice will
be married.

  Please, that's enough,
    huh?

ROSE POME

I'd rather be thin than famous,
I dont wanta be fat,
And a woman throws me outa bed
Callin me Gordo, & everytime
                    I bend
                    to pickup
                    my suspenders
                    from the davenport
                    floor I explode
                    loud huge grunt-o
                    and disgust
                    every one
                    in the familio

   I'd rather be thin than famous
   But I'm fat

Paste that in yr. Broadway Show

BLACK POEM

Self be your lantern,
  Self be your guide—
    Thus spake Tathagata
      Warning of radios
        That would come
        Some day
          And make people
            Listen to automatic
            Words of others

and the general flash of noises,
forgetting self, not-self.—
Forgetting the secret . . . .

Up on high in the mountains so high
  the high magic priests are
    swabbing in the deck
      of broken rib torsos
        cracked in the rack
          of
          Kallaquack
      tryin to figure yr way
      outa the calamity of dust and
      eternity, buz, you better
      get on back to your kind
          b o a t

GRAY POME

Junkies that get too high
Shoot up their old stock of stuff
And sit stupidly on edge
Of bed nodding over
The single sentence in the paper
    They been staring at all night—
    Six, seven hours they'll do this,
    Or get hungup on paragraphs:

"You go on the nod,
    Then you come up,
        Then you start readin
          It again
    Then you go on the nod again
    and everytime you read it
        it gets better"

    You dont remember the next
        rebirth
     but you remember
     the experience

"Took me all evening to read
3 or 4 pages, ossified,
on the nod"

BLUE POEM

The ants are gone asleep
By now, out on those plains
Of pulque and rice
Beyond Pascual
And the Cactus Town
   Matador pan
   Pazatza cuaro
   Mix-technique
   Poop
   Indio
      Yo yo catlepol
      Moon Yowl
      Indian
      Town & City

   Vendors of Take a Giant Step
   Say Hailé
   In back se malleys
   Selling drunks

GREEN POME

             Zoom
             S t a r
          of H o l y
          I n d i a n
     N   I   G   H   T

             The Tathata
                of
             Eminence
                is
             Silence

The Clear Sight
   of Varied Crystal
       Shining Mountains
          shifting in the Air

Exploding Snow

       is Transcendental
       Brilliant Shattered
       Hammered Smithy
       Emerald Green
       Rubioso Mostofo
        Be spark snaked

RED POME

Poppa told me a perfect pome.
It's simple
The smiles of hungry sexy
    brunettes
Looking to lock you in
    lock joint and all
And those eyes of Italian
    deep scenery
In Rivieras of Caviar
    Tree
And Mulberry Bee
    Lampshade
    Sun Ahmenides
    Ahmenemet!
    Ak!
      That's your rosy
       Figury,
            another word
             for future—
That's your come itself

BROWN POME

The reason why there are so many things
Is because the mind breaks it up,
The shapes are empty
That sprung into come
But the mind wont know this
Till a Buddha with golden
Lighted finger, hath pointed
    To the thumb, & made an aphorism
    In a robe on the street,
    That you'll know what it means
    For there to be too many things
    In a world of no-thing.

        One no-thing
        Equals
        All things

When sad sick women
Sing their sex blues
In yr ear, have no fear
    have no fear—
    the moon is true, enough,
    but, but, but, but, but,
    it keeps adding up

WHITE POME

A white poem, a white pure
    spotless poem
    A bright poem
    A nothing poem
    A no-poem non poem
     nondream clean
     silverdawn clear
     silent of birds
     pool-burble-bark
       clear
      the lark of trees
      the needle pines
       the rock the pool
        the sandy shore
      the cleanness of dogs
         the
         frogs
         the
       pure white
       spotless
       Honen
     Honey Land
      Blues

[BIOGRAPHICAL RESUME, FALL 1957]

When I was 4 my brother Gerard was 9, at his deathbed several nuns took down his last words about Heaven and went away with the notes, which I've never seen. They said he was a little saint. My father was a printer, in his plant I often made little one page newspapers, typesetting them and printing them on a hand press (Racetrack News).

I wrote my first novel at age 11, in a 5¢ notebook, about an orphan boy running away, floating down a river in a boat . . . I went to parochial school in little black stockings and pants (St Louis de France & St Joseph in Lowell Mass). In high school, football, which led me (via scouts) to Columbia varsity but I quit football to write (because one afternoon, before scrimmage, I heard Beethoven fifth symphony and it had begun to snow and I knew I wanted to be a Beethoven instead of an athlete) . . . First serious writing at 18, influenced by Hemingway and Saroyan and Whitman . . . . Spent 3 years on first full novel (1100-page Town and City) which was cut to 400 pages by Harcourt-Brace and thereby reduced from a mighty (overlong, windy, but sincere) black book of sorrows into a "saleable" ordinary novel . . . (Never again editorship for me.) My father died in my arms in 1946, alone in house with me, told me to take care of my mother, which I do. After Town and City, I wrote On the Road but it was rejected (1951) so spent 6 years on the road writing whatever came into my head, hopping freights, hitchhiking, working as railroad brakeman, deck hand and scullion on merchant ships, hundreds of assorted jobs, government fire lookout. Slept in mountains and desert in my sleepingbag. My chief activity (seriously) is praying that all living things and all things may go to Heaven. It is said in ancient sutras, that if this prayer and wish is sincere, the deed is already accomplished. I'll buy that.

In recent reading appearance at Village Vanguard I was universally attacked, but all I did was stand there and read my heart out, not caring how I looked or what anybody thought, and I am satisfied because the dishwasher (an old Negro named Elton Stratton) said: "All I wanta do is get 2 quarts of whiskey and lie down in bed and listen to you read to me." Also, the musicians (Lee Konitz, Billy Bauer, Wilbur Little) said I was "singing" when I read and said they heard the music, and since I consider myself a jazz poet, I am satisfied with that. What intelligentsia says makes little difference, as I've always spent my time in skid row or in jazz joints or with personal poet madmen and never cared what "intelligentsia" thinks. My love of poetry is love of joy.

I have been writing my heart out all my life, but only getting a living out of it now, and the attacks are coming in thick. A lot of people are mad and jealous and bitter and I only hope they also can be heard by an expanding publishing program the size of Russia's. Because it's not a question of the merit of art, but a question of spontaneity and sincerity and joy I say. I would like everybody in the world to tell his full life confession and tell it HIS OWN WAY and then we'd have something to read in our old age, instead of the hesitations and cavilings of "men of letters" with blear faces who only alter words that the Angel brought them . . .

As a child, I made long Chaplinesque movies by myself, taking all the parts, silent movies: I began doing this at age 5. Now I write them.

I am only a jolly storyteller and have nothing to do with politics or schemes and my only plan is the old Chinese Way of the Tao: "avoid the authorities." I am a bibulous old jolly drunk and I love everybody.

Jack Kerouac

Dear Don,

Yes, about time for a big hep review.

First, yes, I'll type up a few meditations, and poems, and prose from something. From "Lucien Midnight," my wildprose book, maybe.

Allen Ginsberg: a little prose from his magnificent letter (to me) about Spain, no need to say it's a letter, just prose, would look good alongside his mad new poetry and also introduce his considerable prose ability. Either, or a statement of belief.

Corso: New poetry of his.

Peter Orlovsky: Ginsberg says he has just started writing exceptional and exceptionally strange little poems, Allen is happy about it and says Heaven oped. Allen has these poems in Paris.

Gary Snyder: New poems and a little prose, you might in fact write to Gary (c/o USNS Sappa Creek, Marine Transport Lines, 11 Broadway, NY 4 N.Y.) and ask him to compose a prose explanation of Zen Lunacy which is the backdrop for the Snyder hep shot, very great shot.

Philip Whalen: His address is c/o Judge Richd. Anderson, Lincoln County Courthouse, Newport, Oregon, and he has scads of brilliant poetry and by the way his prose in letters shines. Gary just wrote me and said: "Phil is turning into a beautiful landscape sentient & vast."

Will Petersen: Gary says of him: "Will Petersen is transformation upon transformation, a diamond onion or maybe a growing jewel tree like the Sukhavati says; him & his remarkable wife named Amiko. He wrote a huge stack of letters about love, cooking, No drama, house-cleaning, & his wife's funny winter-girl wool underwear." Maybe you could write Will for something more informal than the Ryoanji garden.

John Clellon Holmes: He is now in London I think, and he has great vocal ability to explain beatness & hipness, maybe you could write him ask for some prose about what he saw of "the angry young men" in England or something but I dont have his English address. His home is Box 167, Old Saybrook, Conn., his mother or sister will forward. His new novel The Horn now being printed at Random, Hiram Haydn's his editor.

Philip Lamantia: Scads of beautiful stuff of all kinds, and he will urge you, as I do, to also publish his brother-poet-ecstatic Howard Hart, a fine new poet. Philip's home is at 1045 Russia St.   San Francisco.

Ed Dorn: A brilliant writer indeed, I'm glad you dug him, he can be reached thru Creeley or Jonathan Williams I guess. Also a great poet, get both prose & poems from him.

Selby Jr.: He's in Brooklyn, our veritable little old Genet tho I've seen greater homosexual prose descriptions etc. by Allen and Burroughs. But Selby is a brave fine writer and his address is 626 Clinton St, Brooklyn.

Robt Creeley: Care/of Gen. Delivery, Alameda, New Mexico, the heppest and very strange writer, tell him to write something about the "new downedness" he calls it. And some poems.

Neal Cassady: I have some prose of his from old letters, describing bums on the railroad, better than mine. (He is "Dean Moriarty")

Mike McClure: Has many strange hep poems, of course, and willing to join in this.

Bill Burroughs: Some weird little piece of his massive work, that would fit in, completing a very hep issue.

Write to me and let me know if, with my own contributions, you want me to send assorted lil pomes by Creeley, McClure, the Cassady prose, the Ginsberg prose, etc. etc. that I have all bundled up here.

See you week of the 24th and give my love to Barney. What I'm glad about The Subterraneans is no hepcat's gonna come up to me and say it's nowhere, it's impossible to call it nowhere, the ordinary readers of course may object to its esoteric style etc.   Till I see you,

                                                        Jack

Why dont you also try to get Koch, O'Hara, Ashbery, and the Marshall of *BMR* #7 and even mebbe a poem by Larry Rivers & a picture of his & a picture by Iris Brodie and a poem by Anton Rosenberg   hep hep one two three!
                              Well, them's the ideas
                              We're living in a wonderful literary
                                    time, actually
(O yes, also I could send you a little masterpiece prose description of the end of the world by Herbert Huncke, the mysterious "Junkey" we never found on Times Square in On the Road, the "Ancke" of Holmes' Go, it is a gem only Ginsberg & I have read & treasured) (Being a down word from the horse's mouth, writ in subway at 5 a m)

A
lil
beato
pome
by
Bob
Lax
Mebbe
too

Dear Don

Well Daddio a sheaf, I think it's a pretty damned nice sheaf and in it you will find a consistency in the prose, and a strange back-and-forth in the poems, to put together a cohesive Beat/Hip thing . . . And since you'll get more material in the mail, from Whalen et al, and maybe a poem by Anton Rosenberg or two, you'll have a rounded out picture. I have taken the pains of typing up this excerpt in here from Burroughs' massive manuscript. Because he cant type himself his manuscripts are well nigh unreadable. I thought it would be a good idea to call it DAYDREAM OF THE DISK, because Burroughs writes what he calls "routines," which are big mad funny satirical daydreams he acts out in front of his friends. In Tangier he never touched a drop till exactly 4 PM, then had his brandy, and started acting out his routines; in the morning, on a little majou, he would then record last night's routines. And because he is a great aristocratic master of the English language, and is really "The Forgotten American," which I can explain later, and because he's been everywhere and done everything, to read his prose is to get a first birds view into the latest accomplishment in human utterance. At least I think so, Don. (I think Burroughs is being put down by publishers for the same reason that he was put down by Peggy Guggenheim and Mary McCarthy when he met them in Venice, he's too frank for society) (polite society as it is?). Daddy Long Legs Burroughs is my way back daddy. He is every bit as great as Céline and greater than Genet, almost; tho he doesnt think so, about Céline I mean, but I'm sure he can do a full narrative job like Céline one of these days and his images are stranger all the time. He stands tragic alone in a sea of facts, all of them strange. He is tall, with thin lips, spectacles, wears gray felt hats and walks down the street with a vigorous pump of his arms like a mad German genius of the 19th century, thru casbahs, medinas & Meixo Thieves Markets of the world. Aint nothin old Bull dont know. Especially now, circa 1958. Ginsberg announced that he has become a Quiet Flowery Sage on top of all that. Whalen says that he is the great ultimate Sanders-of-the-River (no, I said that), Whalen says that he knows the secret of George Sanders vs. Mussolini, or is that Mississippi?

Also, enclosed, fine lil pomes by Mike McClure, a strange pome by Creeley with a dreadful cliche in it ("unquiet dew") but a mysterious poem down further, and you got Neal Cassady's True Prose, which is a new kinda prose, perhaps the finest thing I've sent you . . . and you got Allen Ginsberg's unbelievably wild prose about Breughel painting (with parenthesis of dead cow), and you got other goodies, Lax frinstance, (waitll you dig that!) and you got, best of all, yes now truly this is it, you have the full confession of Herbert Huncke which is going down in history as a classic read by weeping hipsters in Joe's Luncheonette. (Huncke is a reincarnation of Poe, I bet.) And what of mine I sent, may not be what you wanted, if not I'll give you whatever else in town: I put in Some of the Dharma, a page of; and a recent perm from my just-finished book of poems "Orlando Blues"; and a piece of prose (Chapter Fourteen) from "Lucien Midnight" my ultimate nutty masterpiece which has no meaning and therefore opens up the zen gates of cut-link nirvana hey.

Oh yes, finally, to cap everything, write a note
to PETER ORLOVSKY
Box 167
Northport, L.I.
and ask him for his strangest poem.

Save me some of that bourbon, for
a late afternoon chat with witty
Englishmen, how about inviting
Gil Millstein & John Osborne
for a drink (they're looking
for me)

P.S. I deeply appreciate the
beautiful job on The Subterraneans—
thank Barney & you for me—   Jack

[1958]

Dear Don

    Will visit you soon with Allen. Latter sorted through my
papers and found a piece I wrote before "Essentials [of Spon-
taneous Prose]" which is wilder and stranger, and short. En-
closed underneath. You can use that. I'd be sick & tired of
making further big explanations. This can really suffice. I hope
Barney does bring out Mexico City Blues (in entirety, chorus
leading into chorus like jazz), it would sell too. Gregory in
Rome, says he wept in the Colosseum all night and pissed in
Nero's secret cave. Well, here's the early piece on prose: &
format it was in:—

*****BELIEF & TECHNIQUE FOR MODERN PROSE*****

List of Essentials

****

1. Scribbled secret notebooks, and wild typewritten pages, for
   yr own joy
2. Submissive to everything, open, listening
3. Try never get drunk outside yr own house
4. Be in love with yr life
5. Something that you feel will find its own form

46

6. Be crazy dumbsaint of the mind
7. Blow as deep as you want to blow
8. Write what you want bottomless from bottom of the mind
9. The unspeakable visions of the individual
10. No time for poetry but exactly what is
11. Visionary tics shivering in the chest
12. In tranced fixation dreaming upon object before you
13. Remove literary, grammatical and syntactical inhibition
14. Like Proust be an old teahead of time
15. Telling the true story of the world in interior monolog
16. The jewel center of interest is the eye within the eye
17. Write in recollection and amazement for yourself
18. Work from pithy middle eye out, swimming in language sea
19. Accept loss forever
20. Believe in the holy contour of life
21. Struggle to sketch the flow that already exists intact in mind
22. Dont think of words when you stop but to see picture better
23. Keep track of every day the date emblazoned in yr morning
24. No fear or shame in the dignity of yr experience, language & knowledge
25. Write for the world to read and see yr exact pictures of it
26. Bookmovie is the movie in words, the visual American form
27. In Praise of Character in the Bleak inhuman Loneliness
28. Composing wild, undisciplined, pure, coming in from under, crazier the better
29. You're a Genius all the time
30. Writer-Director of Earthly movies Sponsored & Angeled in Heaven

As ever,

Jack

Dear Don

This weekend I want to descend on you with my greatest poem, HEAVEN? (no question mark about that)—will be with Allen G. Could you publish it in next Evergreen Review along with those further notes on spont. writing?

it is really the nicest pome i ever writ. I mean my whole writing-life isnt worth an ash, beside that poem, standing side by side. because it is TRUE.

I had a vision of Heaven. And all is saved.

I had a vision of God's Will.

Who's God?

The Glow Mind started it all, Samsara is a circle begins and ends in the Alaya-Vijnana mind of God or Tathagata. Now I really have something for you, bettern Santa Claus.

Old bean Don, I love you, are we going to publish doctor sax this year? I'd prefer VISIONS OF DEAN. You can make a mint with Visions of Neal Dean. Ray Bremser just wrote to me from Jay City and is a sweet kid from the judge of his kind simple commiserating words. A REAL nice kid, no kidding. Lets not make an issue of his record (like L.).

When Allen G. was here at my home (to which youre invited anytime you wanta make it) he wrote a long beautiful letter to Henry Miller which I thought of sending you for Evergreen then I realized it should at least get to Henry first. Well, who's got anything to hide?

So I sent it to Henry. Later.

I dont care about Henry, you, Allen,
or anybody, I know heaven know heaven now, and that's it.,
and I'll tell you and Barney and the Fillipino Saint in his
Kitchen Why.
Yay.
So, see you this weekend, if I can
find you in. You're swinging. Did you hear
about Rosenthal of Chi Review cant put out me and
Burroughs and poor Dahlberg? Weol, if Ferlinghetti cant
do it too, YOU do it . . . clean up for Barney, because it'll be
NAKED LUNCH, LU   , I mean ALLEN MIDNIGHT
and DHARLBERG
DAHLBERG that is,
great,
andyway, , anyway, I'm stoned,
and write to you,
to let you know I think of you
You turnd
turd

Jack

PS. AM NOW TYPING up my entire
book of sketches, 250 pages of
just as written in breastpocket
notebooks, for 2 years, the
scribblings stranded in streetcorner
riverbottom Mexican California blues
of Oh the white eyes the blue eyes and worn shirts of this good

49 Earl Ave
Northport NY
Oct. 1, 1959

Dear Don

Keep above address a dead secret (only Allen and Sterling know it). Get too much screwy mail and screwy visits. My Ma prefers Northport after all. New little cottage. Florida was a flooded swamp all summer.

Somebody at Grove wrote me a note asking if I liked MexCity Blues appearance of edition, and signed illegible name, so tell whoever it is that of course I love it. The name looks like Martha Schlier or Janet Skler. By the way (I'm out of touch here) let me know reactions to it, or whoever handles that, reviews etc.

Dates:

SAN FRANCISCO BLUES	1954
MEXICO CITY BLUES	1955
SAD TURTLE (Mexcity Blues)	1955
MACDOUGAL ST BLUES	1955
TREE NUMBER TWO	1955
ORIZABA BLUES	1956
MY GANG (same)	
A TV POEM	1958
HEAVEN	1958

Sterling is going to let you have entire VISIONS OF CODY for next big Grove novel by me. Much better than just New Direction "Excerpts"— Plenty time.

I would like a new biography of me for this anthology. Here it is, followed by the poems I remember you also wanted.

****

JACK KEROUAC BIOGRAPHY   After my brother died, when I was four, they tell me I began to sit motionlessly in the parlor, pale and thin, and after a few months of sorrow began to play the old Victrola and act out movies to the music. Some of these movies developed into long serial sagas, "continued next week," leading sometimes to the point where I tied myself with rope in the grass and kids coming home from school thought I was crazy. My brother had taught me how to draw so at the age of 8 I began to produce comic strips of my own: "Kuku and Koko at the Earth's Core," (the first, rudely drawn) on to highly developed sagas like "The Eighth Sea." A sick little boy in Nashua N.H. heard of these and wanted to borrow them. I never saw them again. At the age of eleven I wrote whole little novels in nickel notebooks, also magazines (in imitation of Liberty Magazine) and kept extensive horse racing newspapers going. The first "serious" writing took place after I read about Jack London at the age of 17. Like Jack, I began to paste up "long words" on my bedroom wall in order to memorize them perfectly. At 18 I read Hemingway and Saroyan and began writing little terse short stories in that general style. Then I read Tom Wolfe and began writing in the rolling style. Then I read Joyce and wrote a whole juvenile novel like "Ulysses" called "Vanity of Duluoz." Then came Dostoevsky. Finally I entered a romantic phase with Rimbaud and Blake which I called my "self-ultimacy" period, burning what I wrote in order to be "Self-ultimate." At the age of 24 I was groomed for the Western idealistic concept of letters from reading Goethe's "Dichtung und Wahrheit." The discovery of a style of my own based on spontaneous get-with-it, came after reading the marvelous free narrative letters of Neal Cassady, a great writer who happens also to be the Dean Moriarty of "On the Road." I also learned a lot about unrepressed wordslinging from young Allen Ginsberg and William Seward Burroughs.

Dear Don

Finally, now, for a real crazy gimmick, would you like to have reproduced this cartoon of the Sea-Shroud. It's very beautiful but it was done in ink and crayon on onionskin paper and would be somewhat difficult. I guess you saw it. Allen thinks it great. It could be done panel by panel, instead of full page shrunk, and would give your anthology a wild look. Simply have it photographed by a professional photographer of painting and pastels and prints.

See you soon

As ever,

Jack

Don

My only possible statement on poetics and poetry is this:
Add alluvials to the end of your line when all is exhausted but
something has to be said for some specified irrational reason,
since reason can never win out, because poetry is NOT a sci-
ence. The rhythm of how you decide to "rush" yr statement
determines the rhythm of the poem, whether it is a poem in
verse-separated lines, or an endless one-line poem called prose . .
(with its paragraphs).

So let there be no equivocation about statement, and if
you think this is not hard to do, try it. You'll find that your
lies are heavier than your intentions. And your confessions
lighter than Heaven. .

Otherwise, who wants to read?

I myself have difficulty covering up my bullshit lies

Jack

Dear Don

When I got your letter I promptly started typing up San Francisco Blues in proper chorus form (like Mexico City Blues chorus form) and it was a hell of a job, 79 choruses. I also wrote an introduction explaining the "blues poetry form." The manuscript is dead perfect without a single mistake in it & even contains original lines that I had tried to erase and write over of in 1954! (that's an art in itself)

But, reading the manuscript now—I see it is a beautiful unity. And wouldnt want to send it to you if you only plan to use sections or excerpts of it. As a whole book of poems, it stands right by Mexico City Blues, original, strange, & neat. What do you plan to do with it? What kind of book are you preparing? Something like the Evergreen Anthology? Let me know. Because I hate to see San Francisco Blues be taken apart in pieces. (If you want pieces tell me *how many*, and I could send those—separately.)

. . . . . .

Desolation Angels . . . Sterling has it at the office, we're just holding up on any publication this year (1961) to give the critics a chance to stop saying that I publish too often and give the other books a run. I also have Visions of Gerard (novel) to publish, my best in fact. Gray Williams said he cried when he read it, but wanted "new" novel—. Barney offered a measly $1000 advance for Desolation so we just stored it away. I also plan to print Desolation from the point where I actually sat down to narrative discipline, and remove the first 50 pages which were after all only a mountain diary. This will make Desolation a good package for any publisher. It's after all a big inside novel about Allen, Gregory, Neal, Peter, Lamantia,

Duncan, McClure and all, and about North Beach, the Cellar, etc. Ruth Witt Diamant is even in it.

. . .

My news is that my mother and I moved to Florida a few doors away from her daughter, my sister "Nin," so that I can be freer to travel. And to get me a cabin in the woods somewhere in America soon. We have a brand new house, a private yard with big fences, a supermarket to shop in down the way. These new Fla. houses have wall ovens, heating & airconditioning units, shower stalls, terraza floors, real fawncy and comfortable. You can visit us any time. My mother never forgot "Don" —Memere, that is . . . . Yes, I may go to coast this summer. I just missed you in that bar last summer when I sat that little cat on my lap all night . . . I had a ball that summer time, but overdid it & went a little schizo. (I thought I was being "poisoned by The Subud Cult")!

Don, can you send me a copy of that Ark that already has 2 SF Blues in it? And let me know if you plan to print all 79 choruses of SF Blues, all 40 pages that is. (I've never seen that Ark book). Write soon, I'm taking off right soon (Mexico or someplace). May see you in SF in July or August. I always yearn to go see what old "Dean Moriarty's" up to again . . . . .

Ton ami

Jack

And yearn for Sun Hung Heung's wonton—(& Phil Whalen too) (& Lew Welch)

Allen G's in Cannes with Peter & Gwegowy—headed for Tangiers & Burroughs

Jack Kerouac: SAN FRANCISCO BLUES—In 79 Choruses

San Francisco Blues was my first book of poems, written back in 1954 & hinting the approach of the final blues poetry form I developed for the Mexico City Blues.

In my system, the form of blues choruses is limited by the small page of the breastpocket notebook in which they are written, like the form of a set number of bars in a jazz blues chorus, and so sometimes the word-meaning can carry from one chorus into another, or not, just like the phrase-meaning can carry harmonically from one chorus to the other, or not, in jazz, so that, in these blues as in jazz, the form is determined by time, and by the musician's spontaneous phrasing & harmonizing with the beat of the time as it waves & waves on by in measured choruses.

It's all gotta be non stop ad libbing within each chorus, or the gig is shot.

—Jack Kerouac

[in pencil]   Don—

This is a carefully worded intro to explain, hence revisions—Hope you take good care of these & of yourself

Jack

P.O. Box 700
Orlando, Fla.
Jan. 25 '62

Dear Don
What are you doing with San Francisco Blues? Not a
word from you in 7 months!—
If it's not too late, instead of heading each Chorus "24th
Chorus" etc. just put like
(24)
over the chorus
(25)
etc.
to cut down word strain of writing a number out—
Let me hear—

Jack (Kerouac)

(lost yr. address, robbed)

P.O. Box 700
Orlando Fla.
April 4 1962

Dear Don

Thanx for sending [San Francisco] Blues, I promptly
bound them in my Book of Blues and will leave them there—
Funny how they look so oldfashioned now, they were written
in '54 but now everyone writes like that (with that fuckyou
freedom)—Allen assures me now the avant garde is putting
me down, which is a laugh can be heard even up on Mount
Malaya (which is the mountain where Buddha laughed so much
he busted his sides, before he could settle down and deliver
the Lankavatara Scripture back-and-forth with) (who was it?)
(Mahamati?)—

All this stuff about your anthology ideas evaporating,
in favor of what new concerns? Lawrence Durrell, William
Styron, Snodgrass, Richard Wilbur, Wilbur Maas, John Ciardi,
Robert Frost, Jack Kennedy, Barry Goldwater and William Ful-
bright not to mention Herbert Gold, Gore Vidal, Katherine
Ann Porter (good writer) and Liz Taylor?

God, the whole poetry racket is full of fickle girls.

I'm not interested in what Rumaker's done that I've seen
so far but I do love Selby Junior, Huncke and Rechy too, and
always thought Persky wd. be fine—Creeley's "For Love" I
have, there's not enough swing in it, I think Peter Orlovsky
much better with his harebrained snale graves with grass grow-
ing out of his cock and the grass always greener on the body
in the next graive.

But that'll all come out in the wash, like Smart done,
and Blake—Fox had his day, but Blake groaned on.

Colin Wilson has had to reverse his whole "Outsider"
theory to stay away from me and Allen and Peter and Bill
Burroughs because he probably realizes we'd only pour whiskey
in his hair in the King Lud or King Lull pub . . .

Writers are so evil, nasty, virulent, jealous, shitty—This letter must sound like an outrage from Jack Spicer or that asshole Barker—At least Behan is an honest drinking or non-drinking companion with songs—

Robert Giroux, at Farrar Straus and Cudahy, and I, are together again so we had to bypass Tom Guinzburg as well as your excellent Grove Press associates—It's just a personal old relationship between two old Catholics and I really Don feel good about it—Besides Allen assured me Barney was off me as a writer—So let him publish Jack Gelber and Jerry Tallmer—

Hey! if you have time, send HEAVEN rollscroll poem back too if you can find it, if not, send it back when you get back—This summer I'll be alone in Cornwall (where my ancestors are from, Cornish language is "Kernuak") writing sounds of the Atlantic ocean at Land's End shore . . . then Brittany, Paris, Milano, etc. Funny if we suddenly meet in a Flamenco bar in Cadiz, hey?

Here's to you, sweet Don, and dont stop loving me as I love you, good.

Jack

Memere sends regards to "Don."—

59

GREY FOX BOOKS

Gary Snyder	*He Who Hunted Birds in His Father's Village — Dimensions of a Haida Myth* *Passage Through India* *Riprap & Cold Mountain Poems*
Jack Spicer	*One Night Stand & Other Poems*
Samuel Steward	*Chapters from an Autobiography*
Lew Welch	*How I Work as a Poet & Other Essays* *I Leo — An Unfinished Novel* *I Remain: The Letters of Lew Welch with the Correspondence of His Friends* *Ring of Bone, Collected Poems* *Selected Poems*
George Whitmore	*The Confessions of Danny Slocum*
Philip Whalen	*Decompressions, Selected Poems* *Enough Said, Poems 1974–1979* *Scenes of Life at the Capital*
Roy F. Wood	*Restless Rednecks, Gay Tales of a Changing South*
Allen Young	*Gays Under the Cuban Revolution*